The Mommy Cup

Written and illustrated by

Heather Ruskievicz

Balboa Press books may be ordered through booksellers or by contacting:

Balboa Press
A Division of Hay House
1663 Liberty Drive
Bloomington, IN 47403
www.balboapress.com
1-(877) 407-4847

Rudolph Uhlman Photography

ISBN: 978-1-4525-7985-6 (sc)
ISBN: 978-1-4525-7986-3 (e)

Library of Congress Control Number: 2013914482

Printed in the United States of America.

Balboa Press rev. date: 11/1/2013

BALBOA
PRESS
A DIVISION OF HAY HOUSE

Foreword

"The Mommy Cup" provides a two-fold message for families with very young children. In very simple language it teaches children that mothers need time for restoration and refueling.

First, it introduces young children to the concept that mothers do many things in the home beside tend to the needs of the children. Empathy and caring behaviors are suggested for children and their fathers to follow in support of their mother and wife.

Secondly, it teaches mothers the importance of self-care as it validates their need to take time out for themselves. The story lends itself to a follow-up family discussion for how they can help refill one another's cup in healthy ways.

Sally DeSpain, MA,
Child Mental Health Specialist

Dedication

This book is dedicated to all those who take care of others, especially my four moms; E-Mom, Nancy, Ditty and Gaby.

One birthed me, one raised me, one inspired me, and one lent me her son.

And of course, my husband Steve, and daughter Shelby. Thank you for putting up with me when I'm off chasing the next great adventure!

Inspiration

My wicked, evil step-mother (as she used to call herself and then we would laugh ourselves silly) used to regularly ask me how full my cup was. She knew only too well most of any time left after family and work got filled up with helping others. She would ask me what I had done lately for myself and if a good answer wasn't forthcoming I would get "the look". And then of course she would laugh because that's what she and I did together. After spending time with her one afternoon I came home and the idea for *The Mommy Cup* popped into my head. I realized that it was important to share this because not everyone is blessed with a wonderful wicked, evil stepmother like I was. In the past ten years my son died, I spent three years constructing the building for my bakery business, started the bakery, said farewell to my wicked stepmother, had a stroke and recently found out I am allergic to almost everything I work with at the bakery. Through all of this I have indeed learned to check the level in my cup. I hope you do too.

Once upon a time there was a Mommy named Maria. She lived in a yellow farmhouse with her six children. This family had a Daddy too, named Stan. They were a very special family. Maria was kept very busy every day. Because they lived on a farm she had lots of things to do.

Goats to milk.

Chickens to feed. And eggs to find.

During the spring there were seeds to plant. And in the summer

and fall there were many crops to pick, and dry, and can.

And wood to split and stack.

During the winter there was snow to be shoveled. And snowsuits to put on and take off. And boots and mittens to put on… and take off...

And Christmas presents to be wrapped and hidden. And the Christmas tree had to be cut and decorated!

And in between all this there were owies to mend for J.J.

And dolls to fix for Kira and Karen. And 4H and scouts for

Donovan and Marta. And nursing Ella.

Of course Maria liked to take time out for her husband Stan too, who worked very hard building houses.

One day J.J. came to Maria with an extra big owie. In the background Karen and Kira were fighting over a toy.

Then Marta started whining that she was hungry.

And one of the dogs starting barking.

Maria did something that she really didn't like to do. From way down deep this little voice crawled out and by the time it fell out of her mouth it was very loud!

She actually yelled at Marta. And felt very badly about it.

She fixed J.J.'s boo-boo and then went to the cupboard to get

out her mommy cup. It felt very light. She looked inside of it.

There was dust in it! It was completely empty!

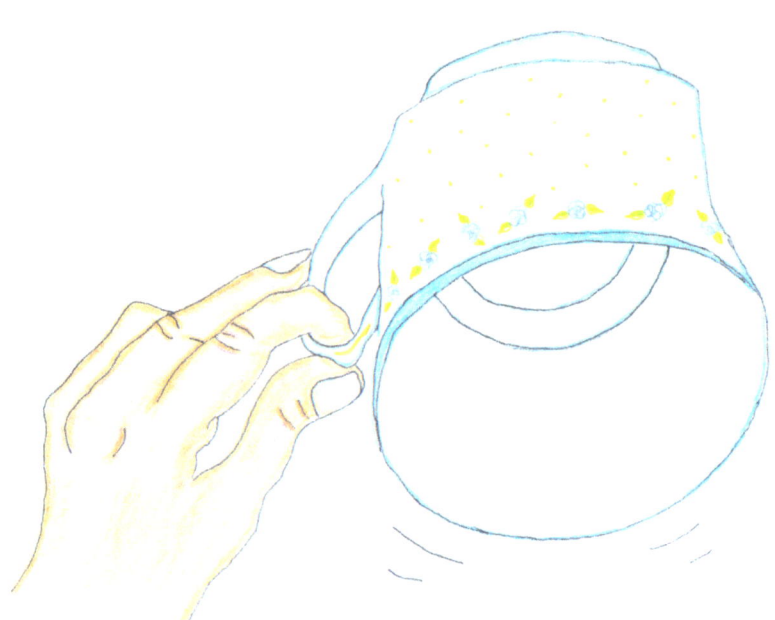

Not one single drop.

She sat down in her favorite chair. She held the mommy cup in her hands. Marta came over. "What's that?" Marta asked. It was hard to explain. "Well," she said, "every time I help someone out I use a little bit out of my cup. When I do something for me a little bit fills back up."

Marta looked at the cup and then looked back at her mom. "You haven't been doing anything for yourself Mommy. Is that why you yelled at me?" Maria nodded slowly. "That could be."

Marta put her arms around her mommy's neck and hugged her. "I'm sorry Mommy. I love you." Then something happened! Marta and Maria looked down in the cup. In the very bottom was a tiny drop.

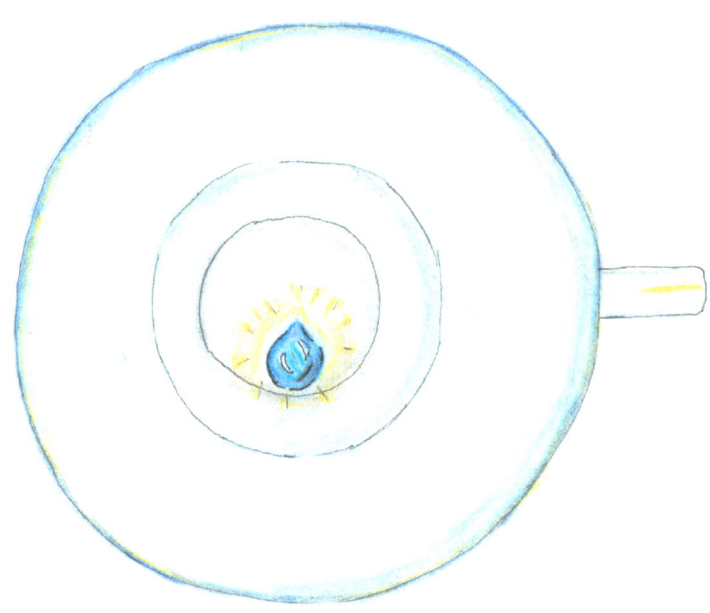

"Maybe you should go take a bubble bath, Mommy", Marta suggested. Maria thought about it. Ella was sleeping, the two four year olds were playing quietly now and J.J. was watching cartoons.

"I think I will just do that" she said to Marta and marched off to the bathroom. Marta heard the water running and watched as the level in the mommy cup came up just a bit. Maria snuggled down in the bubbles and sighed. It felt glorious! She closed her eyes and smiled to herself.

All of a sudden, Plop! Plop! Splash! Karen and Kira had jumped in the tub with her. They giggled.

She sighed again and got out and dried off. Marta sighed as the mommy cup level went back to one drop.

That night after dinner Marta crawled into her daddy's lap.

"We need to help Mommy" she whispered to him.

"Oh? How is that?" he asked her.

Marta explained about the mommy cup and that Mommy wasn't as happy as she usually was. Daddy thought about this for awhile and told Marta he would see what he could do.

The next afternoon a friend of Maria's arrived at her front door. She had a pink bow on her head!

"A present from Stan" she said. "I'm here for two hours, so go do something just for you."

"But Ella might want to eat!" Maria said.

"I'll take care of Ella Mae" her friend replied.

"But the girls just started baking cookies" Maria protested.

"We'll manage. Now, where are your boots? Here's your jacket. Now go out for a walk. That's an order!"

Maria knew she was over powered. She grabbed a Parents magazine.

"Oh no you don't", her friend chided her. "This is time for you, not for children".

"But…"

"No buts, now scoot!"

So Maria put on her jacket and went outside. She started walking down the driveway. It was so quiet. Then she noticed a bird chirping. Then another.

She inhaled deeply. She could smell freshly mown hay. The sky was so blue! She looked around. It all was so pretty! She walked for awhile and then sat down under one of their apple trees.

She closed her eyes for a few minutes.

With a start she awoke! She looked at her watch. She had napped for an hour and a half! She got up and walked home. When she walked inside the aroma of freshly baked cookies greeted her.

Her friend was sitting on the floor with Ella in her lap, reading a story to the other children. As she came in the door they ran over to her and greeted her with hugs and kisses. Maria gave her friend a big hug as she walked out the door.

"So Maria, I'll see you next week."

She followed her and stood outside talking for a few minutes. Maria looked at her and said, "That was wonderful, but I feel so guilty about just going off and doing nothing."

Her friend looked her square in the eye. "Maria, do those children look the worse for wear?"

Did the house come crashing down?" Maria shook her head "Do you feel more relaxed?" Maria nodded. "What would happen if something happened to you? Would the dishes still get done, meals cooked, laundry washed?

Yes, they would. Everyone would miss you and miss your love, but things would carry on. None of us are indispensable. Moms are extra special because they play so many roles. Just like a car that needs gas to go, moms need to fuel themselves. Not only with food, but emotionally too. That means taking time out for you. Not with the kids, but by yourself. Then when you come back you'll have more to give."

Maria thought about the mommy cup. She walked back inside and looked at the little cup sitting on the counter. It was half-full.

Never again, she thought, never again will I let my cup become empty. And she settled down on the couch, gathered her children around her and finished reading the story.

The End

Author's Note

Or, perhaps the beginning of your new story. Do you have a "mommy cup"? If so, how full is it? If you take time to help other people (or animals) then you need to take time to nurture yourself too. Not someday, but now. It is not selfish or self-centered to take time to nourish yourself. Do you make sure that your car has enough gas, the tires are properly inflated and the oil is changed (in my case fairly) regularly? Why should you treat yourself any less importantly than a vehicle? But yet we tend to. Don't wait for a catastrophic health condition to get your attention! Take time now. Find something that would fill your "mommy cup" and then go do it. Please.

Warmest regards, Heather

www.ingramcontent.com/pod-product-compliance
Lightning Source LLC
Chambersburg PA
CBHW060818290526
45792CB00005BB/1707